SCHOLASTIC GUIDES

PUNCTUATION POWER

Punctuation and How to Use It

Marvin Terban

SCHOLASTIC
REFERENCE

For Karen, David, and Jennifer:
You punctuate my life!

Library of Congress Cataloging-in-Publication Data

Terban, Marvin.
    Punctuation power/by Marvin Terban.
       p. cm.—(Scholastic guides)
    Includes index.
    Summary: Explains the purpose and importance of punctuation and how it is used, covering apostrophes, colons, commas, exclamation points, hyphens, parentheses, slashes, and more.
    1. English language—Punctuation—Handbooks, manuals, etc.—Juvenile literature. [1. English language—Punctuation.]
    I. Title. II. Series.
    PE1450.T47   2000
    428.2—dc21   99-19179
                                      CIP

ISBN 0-590-38673-5

10 9 8 7 6 5 4 3 2 1   0/0 01 02 03 04

Book design by Nancy Sabato
Composition by Brad Walrod
Cover and interior illustrations by Eric Brace
Printed in the U.S.A.   23
First printing, March 2000

Table of Contents

PART TWO

Introduction

WHY IS PUNCTUATION IMPORTANT?

Imagine trying to read something that didn't have any punctuation marks, capital letters, or correct spacing. It would be very tricky. You wouldn't know when sentences and paragraphs began or ended. You wouldn't know when to take those little pauses that help divide sentences into separate thoughts. You wouldn't know which sentences were stating facts, asking questions, giving orders, or expressing strong emotions. It would be a mess. Try it and see.

> my favorite neighbor mrs freedman she just moved here from massachusetts asked me to go to the store and get her a lot of things crayons paper scissors and glue she told me i want to draw some pictures wow thats great where should i go i asked just to the corner store she said but you mustnt dilly dally waste time because the store closes at 600 pm you can count on me i shouted as i ran out the door

Now here's the same passage with punctuation marks, capital letters, and spacing.

> My favorite neighbor, Mrs. Freedman (she just moved here from Massachusetts), asked me to go to the store and get her a lot of things: crayons, paper, scissors, and glue. She told me, "I want to draw some pictures."
>
> "Wow! That's great. Where should I go?" I asked.
>
> "Just to the corner store," she said, "but you mustn't dilly-dally [waste time] because the store closes at 6:00 p.m."

"You can count on me!" I shouted as I ran out the door.

See how much easier it was to read?

Punctuation marks, capital letters, and spacing are like sign-posts. They are symbols that help guide us through written language. They give us clues about the thoughts and feelings of the writer. They help us to avoid confusion and to understand more clearly what the writer is trying to say to us.

Think about the next four sentences.

To Amanda Justin is a great brother.
When he walked in in his costume the
  audience roared.
Those who can climb mountains on
  stilts.
Aaron was teasing his goldfish and his
  cat bit him.

Now, just add commas, and the meanings become clear.

To Amanda, Justin is a great brother.
When he walked in, in his costume, the audience roared.
Those who can, climb mountains on stilts.
Aaron was teasing his goldfish, and his cat bit him.

The punctuation mark at the end of a sentence makes a lot of difference, too.

I won. (The person is stating a fact.)
I won! (The person is very excited.)
I won? (The person can't believe it.)

As you see, the final punctuation mark tells you the feeling the writer wanted to express when he/she wrote each sentence.

If you want to be a better writer and communicate your ideas more clearly, you need punctuation marks, capital letters, and good spacing. You can't do without them. This book will give you punctuation power and help you to be a more perfect punctuator.

HOW TO USE THIS BOOK

To learn how to use punctuation marks correctly, you can look them up in this book in four different ways.

There's a **Table of Contents** for the whole book on page 3. It lists all the parts and sections in the order that they appear. Just glance down the Table of Contents until you find the number of the page on which the part you want begins. Turn there and skim through the pages that follow until you find the information you're looking for.

If you want to know all about a specific punctuation mark, turn to the special Table of Contents for **Part One: Punctuation and How to Use It** on page 8. Each punctuation mark has its own section with explanations and examples. The punctuation marks are listed in alphabetical order followed by the page number each section starts on. (The other major parts of the book also have their own Table of Contents pages.)

If you have a question about a very specific punctuation rule, look in the **Index** at the end of the book starting on page 95.

For a quick browse, you can flip through the book and use the **tabs** on the edges of the pages. Stop when you get to the section you want.

There is also a **Glossary** beginning on page 92 that defines many of the grammar terms and other tricky words in this book.

Not all writers follow exactly the same rules of punctuation. Sometimes two writers will punctuate the same sentence differently, and both will be right. This book will point out when you have choices. You can then decide for yourself what to do, but remember to be consistent. Always follow the same rules throughout your paper.

Part One

PUNCTUATION AND HOW TO USE IT

Apostrophes

Apostrophes are used in three important ways:

1. in possessive nouns
2. in contractions
3. to make letters, signs, symbols, and numbers plural

Use apostrophes to make nouns possessive.

"To possess" means "to own." So possessive nouns show ownership.

People sometimes ask: If you write or say, "Tyrone's wife is a doctor," does Tyrone really "own" or "possess" his wife? Of course not. So you have to think of possessive nouns as sometimes expressing a very close relationship as well as actual ownership.

SINGULAR POSSESSIVE NOUNS

Add 's to make any singular noun possessive.

The bird's wings were green and blue.
Monica's hat blew across the street.

What if the singular noun already ends with the letter **s**, or even **ss**? Stick to the rule: Add **'s** to any singular noun to make it possessive.

The bus's door got stuck, and I couldn't get off.
Do not disturb the genius's experiment.
The walrus's tusk is a long, pointed tooth.
I borrowed my boss's car and dented it!
The waitress's tray crashed to the floor.

The jury was shocked by the witness's testimony.
My class's project won first prize.

What if the singular noun is a proper noun and ends with **s**? Stick to the rule: Add **'s** to make any singular noun possessive.

Mr. Barnes's history test was hard but fair.
Dennis's sister is Charles's wife and James's daughter.
Charles Dickens's books include *A Christmas Carol*
   and *Oliver Twist.*
Sherlock Holmes's rooms were on Baker Street in London.
Virgil wrote about Aeneas's adventures after the
   Trojan War.
Paris's boulevards are wide and beautiful.

If a word like "Paris's" sounds too hissy to you, you can write "the boulevards of Paris."

Some writers today feel that adding **'s** to a singular noun that already ends with **s** or **ss** is not necessary. These writers feel that just the apostrophe alone is enough, especially if the noun is a proper noun or has more than one syllable. In the sample sentences above, these writers would probably write waitress', witness', Barnes', Dennis', Charles', James', Dickens', Holmes', and Aeneas'. You can do that too, or you can stick to the old rule (add **'s** to make any singular noun possessive). Either way, you will be right. Whichever way you do it, always do it the same way.

PLURAL POSSESSIVE NOUNS

**If the last letter of a plural noun is _s_, just add
an apostrophe to make the noun possessive.**

**If the last letter of a plural noun is
not _s_, add 's to make the noun possessive.**

Plural nouns that end with the letter *s*	Possessive forms (add just an apostrophe)
babies	babies'
dogs	dogs'
teachers	teachers'
girls	girls'

Plural nouns that don't end with the letter *s*	Plural possessive forms (add *'s*)
men	men**'s**
children	children**'s**
deer	deer**'s**
mice	mice**'s**
geese	geese**'s**

Possessive *nouns* always have apostrophes.

> boy's, Bill's, cats', queen's, Ms. Jones's

Possessive *pronouns* never have apostrophes.

> yours, hers, its, ours, theirs
> *Yours* has green polka dots. *Hers* has purple stripes.
> The kitten forgot where it left *its* toy.
> *Ours* is twice as big as *theirs*.

MAKING COMPOUND NOUNS POSSESSIVE

Add **'s** to the last word in a compound noun to make it possessive.

> The Queen of England**'s** palace is very elegant.
> She ate all of her father-in-law**'s** chocolate cookies.

The editor in chief's face grew red when he saw the silly headline.

(See *Compound Words* on page 54.)

SPECIAL RULES ABOUT POSSESSIVE NOUNS

If two or more people own the same thing or have a special relationship with the same person, make only the last person possessive.

I borrowed Aaron, Jessica, and Jade's pet kangaroo.
Harriet and Lenny's daughters all work at the zoo.

If two or more people own different things, make all the separate nouns that show ownership possessive.

Judi's and Gerry's dogs won medals. (Judi and Gerry own different dogs that were prize-winners.)
The Leongs' and Westermans' houses were not damaged by the hurricane. (Each house is owned by a different family.)

CONTRACTIONS

Use an apostrophe in a contraction to show where the missing letter or letters used to be.

When you squeeze two words together into one word and leave out one or more letters, you make a *contraction*. ("To contract" means "to shorten.") Put the apostrophe where the missing letters used to be.

The two words being contracted are usually

a **pronoun** + a **verb** (I + will = I'll) or
a **verb** + "not" (did + not = didn't).

COMMON CONTRACTIONS

aren't = *are not*
can't = *cannot*
couldn't = could *not*
could've = *could have*
didn't = *did not*
doesn't = *does not*
don't = *do not*
hadn't = *had not*
hasn't = *has not*
haven't = *have not*
he'd = *he would, he had*
he'll = *he will*
he's = *he is*
I'd = *I would, I had*
I'll = *I will*
I'm = *I am*
isn't = *is not*
it's = *it is, it has*
I've = *I have*
let's = *let us*
mightn't = *might not*
might've = *might have*
mustn't = *must not*
needn't = *need not*
shan't = *shall not* (rare)

she'd = *she would, she had*
she'll = *she will*
she's = *she is*
shouldn't = *should not*
should've = *should have*
they'd = *they would, they had*
they'll = *they will*
they're = *they are*
they've = *they have*
wasn't = *was not*
we'd = *we would, we had*
we'll = *we will*
we're = *we are*
weren't = *were not*
we've = *we have*
who'd = *who would, who had*
who's = *who is, who has*
who'll = *who will*
won't = *will not*
wouldn't = *would not*
would've = *would have*
you'd = *you would, you had*
you'll = *you will*
you're = *you are*
you've = *you have*

In informal writing (like letters or e-mails to friends), or when you write dialogue (and you try to write words as real people might actually pronounce them), you can use contractions like those below. Just remember to put an apostrophe where the missing letter or letters used to be even if you are shortening a single word (example: *them* to *'em*). And try not to overdo it.

> What'll we do now?
> That'll be the day.
> Kai-Fai's surfing the Internet in his room.
> When's the game?
> Where'd my money go?
> What'd you say? That'd be fine!
> I like 'em with ketchup, not mustard.
> They were dancin' and singin' all night long!

It's *have,* not *of.*

When you hear someone say *could've* or *should've* or *would've*, you might think that the end of the word sounds like *of.* Just remember that *'ve* at the end of these contractions is short for *have.* So write "I could **have** done that," and never "I could of done that."

Don't confuse *its* with *It's.*

Its is a possessive pronoun that means "belongs to it." This word never has an apostrophe.

> My rabbit can't find its rubber carrot anywhere.

It's is the contraction for "it is" or "it has." It always stands for two words, and it always has an apostrophe.

> It's (it is) hanging in the closet next to the turkey.

It's (it has) been very nice meeting you, Mr. Dracula.

If you can't decide whether to use *it's* or *its*, say the sentence to yourself, but instead of saying *its*, say "it is" or "it has." If one of those sounds right, use *it's*. Otherwise, use *its*.

The dog buried ___?___ bone.

Say, "The dog buried it is bone. The dog buried it has bone." Both those sentences sound wrong, so write *its*.

___?___ going to rain today.

Say, "It is going to rain today." That sounds good, so use *it's*.

Remember: *It's* always takes the place of two words: "it is" or "it has." It's easy. Yes, it is!

Don't confuse *whose* with *who's*.

Whose is a possessive pronoun. It always shows ownership, and it never has an apostrophe.

The artist whose painting fell off the wall is furious. (The artist *owns* the painting.)
I would like to know whose dirty socks are on my sandwich. (Someone *owns* those socks.)

Who's is a contraction for "who is" or "who has." It always takes the place of two words, and it always has an apostrophe.

Will the person who's (who is) hiding in the mummy case
please come out now.

"Who's (who has) been sitting in my chair?" growled Papa
Bear.

If you are not sure whether to write *who's* or *whose*, substitute "who is" or "who has" for the word you're wondering about. If one of those sounds right, then write *who's*. Otherwise, write *whose*.

I gave the gerbil to the boy __?__ hamster ran away.

Say, "I gave the gerbil to the boy who is hamster ran away. I gave the gerbil to the boy who has hamster ran away." Those don't sound right, so write *whose*. Remember, *whose* shows ownership. The boy owned the hamster.

Don't confuse *your* with *you're*.

Your is a possessive pronoun. It always shows ownership, and it never has an apostrophe.

Please get your sloppy feet off the new kitchen table!
Your frog is hopping around and annoying the parrot.

You're is a contraction. It always takes the place of two words, "you are," and it always has an apostrophe.

You're (you are) cute, even though you're a gremlin.
Mom says you're (you are) in big trouble for putting bubble
bath in the washing machine.

If you can't decide whether to write *your* or *you're*, substitute "you are" for the word in question. If "you are" sounds right, then write *you're*. Otherwise, write *your*.

__?__ right.

Say, "You are right." That sounds OK. So write *you're*.

Don't confuse *lets* with *let's*.

Lets is the present tense of the verb "to let." It means "allows" or "permits." Used this way, "lets" does not have an apostrophe.

> Grandma always lets us play with her stuffed dinosaurs.

Let's is a contraction. It always takes the place of two words, "let us," and it always has an apostrophe.

> Let's (let us) ask Grandma where her stuffed dinosaurs are.

If you can't decide whether *lets* or *let's* belongs in your sentence, say the sentence with "let us." If that sounds right, then use "let's." Otherwise, use "lets."

> Our teacher never ___?___ us talk during a test.
> Our teacher never let us us talk during a test.

That sounds wrong, so write *lets*.

Put an apostrophe in the contractions of years.

If you leave out the first two numbers in a year (the numbers that tell the century), put an apostrophe where those numbers used to be. If there might be confusion about what century you mean, write the full year out with all four numbers.

> The Class of '50 is holding its reunion in the gym.
> The tornado flattened the town in the summer of '99.
> We dressed up as the Spirit of '76 for the Fourth of July parade.

Use apostrophes to make letters, numbers, symbols, signs, and punctuation marks plural.

Sometimes when you are writing, you have to make something plural that isn't a word. Here's how to do it.

Add 's to make a letter plural.

> Mrs. Krosstoffminoff spells her name with two s's, three o's, and four f's.
> Your a's look just like your u's because you don't close the tops.
> Her handwriting is weird. She dots her e's and crosses her b's.

Add 's or just s to make a number or a decade plural.

Today writers do it both ways. It's your choice, but be consistent. Always do it the same way.

With an Apostrophe:

In the late 1960's, American astronauts went to the moon.
Does your phone number have two 4's or three?

Without an Apostrophe:

In the late 1990s, people looked forward to the twenty-first century.
Please cut out more 6s for the math bulletin board.

Add 's to make a symbol, sign, or punctuation mark plural.

> There are too many #'s, &'s, and !'s on this poster.
> The math teacher says I make my ='s crooked.
> Ying-Ying sometimes forgets to put @'s in her e-mail addresses.

Brackets

Brackets look like parentheses, but they're straight, not curved.

Use brackets inside quotations

1. to add information in your own words.
2. around your own words that fill in missing words when you shorten a quote.
3. to show that you are quoting someone else's mistake without correcting it.

Use brackets around your own words that you have inserted into the words of someone you are quoting.

When you are quoting someone and you want to insert your own comments, put your words into brackets. There are many reasons why you may want to add your own words to someone else's:

1. to explain or describe something
2. to give extra information
3. to correct a mistake

"When she saw him [the man with the beard], she handed him the package, and dashed out," announced the spy.

"Julius Caesar [100–44 B.C.] was a great, but controversial, Roman leader," said the guest speaker.

The newspaper reported, "The kids have voted Miss Y. [Karen Youngman, the special ed instructor] Teacher of the Year."

Our new history book contained the following sentence:
"William Henry Harrison, the eighth [actually, the ninth] President of the United States, died in 1842 [actually,

1841] after only one year [it was one month] in office."
That proves that even books can get their facts wrong.

When you use brackets this way, you are telling the reader that the words in the brackets are yours, not those of the source you are quoting. You are adding your own words to make the sentence clearer, to give additional facts, or to correct a fact that is wrong. The brackets separate your words from those of the quoted person.

Use brackets around your own words that fill in missing words when you shorten a quote.

Sometimes you have to shorten a long quote to make it fit your paper. But you may have to add a few words of your own to make the shortened passage smoother to read. Put brackets around your words to separate them from the quoted words.

Original full quote:

"Benjamin Franklin (1706–90) was a statesman, scientist, author, editor, publisher, printer, and inventor. He helped the thirteen original colonies win the American Revolution. He signed the Declaration of Independence (1776), the Treaty of Paris (1783), and he helped draft the Constitution of the United States (1787–89). His many well-known inventions include a stove, bifocal eyeglasses, and the lightning rod."

Shortened quote with added words in brackets:

"Benjamin Franklin (1706–90) was a statesman, scientist, author, editor, publisher, printer, and inventor... [of the Franklin] stove, bifocal eyeglasses, and the lightning rod."

The writer cut forty-one words out of the quotation and added three new words to make exactly the sentence needed for the paper.

Use brackets around the word *sic*.

Use brackets to enclose the word *sic* in a quotation right after a word that has a mistake in it (like the wrong spelling) or after an error of fact. *Sic* means "thus" or "so" in Latin, and it shows that you are repeating someone else's mistake in a direct quotation on purpose and not making a mistake of your own. (Note: the word *sic* is always in italics.)

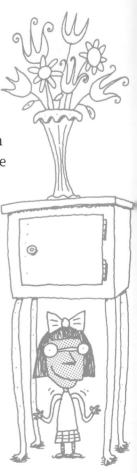

> On her test she wrote, "Abraham Linkun [*sic*] wore a tall silk hat during the Civil War."
> "Sybil is adorably short—barely fifty [*sic*] feet tall."

Use brackets around stage directions in a script.

You can use brackets in the script of a play around stage directions that are usually typed in italics. This shows the actors what they should do or how they should act.

> JENNIFER: [*hysterically throwing her plate on the floor*] I will never eat meat again! Never! Never!

Stage directions in a script can also be put into parentheses or printed in italics without brackets or parentheses. It depends on who is typing the script. (See *Play Scripts* on page 89.)

Capital Letters

Capitalize the first word in a sentence.

The bunny ate too much, got dizzy, and fell off the sofa.

Capitalize the pronoun *I*.

He had the nerve to say that I sang off key—I, who took singing lessons with Madame Margo for five years!

Capitalize proper nouns (names of specific people, places, and things).

Roslyn Penn
Columbia Prep School
Brooklyn, New York
Rocky Mountains

Capitalize proper adjectives.

Proper adjectives come from proper nouns.

Proper Noun	Proper Adjective
America	American
Switzerland	Swiss
Japan	Japanese
Norway	Norwegian
Argentina	Argentine or Argentinean
Florida	Floridian
Boston	Bostonian

Capitalize ideas and abstract nouns when they are used as proper nouns for special effect (sometimes in poems, speeches, fables, myths, fairy tales, names of paintings, words of songs, or folktales).

O, Freedom, how we do cherish thee!
What is life without Liberty?
And then Mercy whispered tenderly, "I grant you pardon."

Capitalize official titles or positions when they come in front of a person's name.

Dr. Albert Schweitzer
General Ulysses S. Grant
Ms. Lorrie Gerson
Captain Sue Kilmer

Vice President Margaret Scotto
Chief Justice John Marshall
Prime Minister Margaret Thatcher
Professor Anthony Barnes

Capitalize important titles, even if the person's name is not mentioned.

The President of the United States went to the circus.
The Prime Minister forgot his hat at the conference.
We will have to consult the Secretary of
    Education on this.

Capitalize official titles when they are used without the person's name if you are speaking or writing directly to that person.

I must request, Judge, that you stop
    chewing on the gavel.
Yes, Governor, I'll wipe the
    mustard off your tie
    immediately.
The war is that way, General.

Look, Your Majesty, a hideous dragon is knocking at the gates
of your castle. Shall I serve tea?

**Capitalize abbreviations of
titles after someone's name.**

Martin Luther King, Jr.
Esther Brill, Ph.D.
Jason Brett, M.D.

**Capitalize the titles of family members
when they are used with their names.**

Aunt Rozzie, Grandpa Lester, Cousin Judi, Uncle Daisuke

**Capitalize the titles of family members if you are speaking
or writing directly to them, even if you don't use their names.**

Thanks for the beautiful iguana, Grandma.
Oh, Mom and Dad, this is my new boyfriend, Rocko.

**Capitalize the titles of specific family members if you are
speaking about them without using their names.
(It's as if their titles are their names.)**

I heard Grandma tell Dad that she had bought Mom a new
armadillo and that Grandpa was jealous.

Capitalize the days of the week.

Monday, Tuesday, Wednesday, etc.

Capitalize the months of the year.

January, February, March, etc.

Do *not* capitalize the names of the seasons.

summer, fall, autumn, winter, spring

Capitalize the first word in the greeting (salutation) of a friendly letter.

My dear Angelo,   Hi, George,
Hello, Sayaka,   Dearest nephew Justin,
Dear Loraine,   Darling Amanda,

Capitalize the first word and all the main words in the greeting (salutation) of a business letter.

Dear Members of the Improvement Committee:
Dear Sir or Madam:
To Whom It May Concern:
Dear Customer Service Department:

Capitalize the first word in the closing of any letter, friendly or business.

Warmest wishes,   Your obedient servant,
Best regards,   Very truly yours,
Sincerely yours,   Fondly,
Love,   Respectfully,

Capitalize the first, last, and all the main words in the title of a

book: *The Secret Garden*
movie: *Star Wars*
song: "This Land Is My Land"
play: *The Taming of the Shrew*
musical show: *The Lion King*

opera: *The Marriage of Figaro*
magazine: *Highlights for Children*
newspaper: *The New York Times*
television show: *I Love Lucy*
radio program: *World News Tonight*

Do not capitalize a short word (like *the*, *a*, *an*, *of*, *in*, *by*, or *for*) unless it is the first or last word in a title.

For Whom the Bell Tolls   *The Wizard of Oz*
Of Mice and Men   *Time Goes By*
A Tale of Two Cities   *Jumping In*

Capitalize the first word in every line of poetry.

Birds, birds everywhere,
In the trees and in my hair;
Birds are fowl, but some are fair;
A bird is sitting in my chair!

Capitalize the names of languages.

French, Latin, Spanish

Capitalize the names of school subjects when they are specific courses listed in a school or college catalog. (Capitalize the first, last, and all important words.)

Environmental Issues   Greek and Roman Comedy
World History 101   Introduction to Advanced Math
Kitchen Chemistry   Painting and Drawing
Computer Repairs   Long-lost Literature

Do not capitalize school subjects that are not languages or specific courses in a school catalog or college listing.

math	geography
science	music
history	physical education
biology	art

Capitalize geographic locations when they refer to specific places on the map or sections of a country, not just directions.

Specific geographic locations (capitalize the first letter):

Henny went out West to seek his fortune in oil wells.
Sun-Sook Kim and Alan moved from the North to the South.
Many great colleges are located in the East.
The Southwest can be very hot.

Directions (do not capitalize):

Drive south for two miles. Turn east at the traffic light and go one block. Drive north for two blocks. Turn west at the fountain, and you'll find the restaurant. But it's closed.

Capitalize holidays, festivals, and special events (national, regional, local, neighborhood, school, and religious).

All Saints' Day	Labor Day
Christmas	Memorial Day
Broadway Street Fair	Monte Azul
Columbus Day	National Dog Week
Easter	Passover
Eid el-Fitr	Rosh Hashanah
Flag Day	Saint Patrick's Day
Good Friday	Shavuot

Halloween   Saint Andrew's Day
Hanukkah   Sukkot
Homecoming Weekend   Thanksgiving
Id al-Adha   Valentine's Day
Id al-Fitr   Veterans Day
Kwanzaa   Yom Kippur

Capitalize religions, tribes, ethnic groups, and nationalities.

African, Apache, Asian, Aztec, Buddhist, Caucasian,
  Cherokee, Christian, Hindu, Hispanic, Hopi, Irish-American,
  Islam, Israeli, Japanese, Jewish, Muslim, Pueblo, Romanian,
  Russian, Spanish, Swahili

Capitalize gods and goddesses and holy books and documents.

Allah	Brahma	Buddha	Vishnu
Bible	God	the Koran	New Testament
Old Testament	Shiva	Talmud	Torah

**Capitalize the names of all the planets in the
solar system, including Earth (but not *sun* or *moon*).**

Jupiter, the largest planet, has many moons.
The goddess of love and a planet are both named Venus.
There is more water than earth on the planet Earth, so our
  planet should be named Ocean.

Remember: The third planet from the sun is Earth, a proper noun
that should be capitalized. Soil and dirt are earth.

Capitalize historical periods and events.

the Great Depression   the Renaissance

the Middle Ages
the Revolutionary War

the Industrial Revolution
Reconstruction

Capitalize brand names of products.

Nintendo, Tylenol, Nike, Play-Doh, Kodak, Kleenex

Capitalize names of companies, stores, and businesses.

Apple Computer, Inc.
Ford Motor Company
Procter & Gamble

New Balance Athletic Shoe, Inc.
The Gap
Starbucks

Capitalize the first word in a direct quotation.

The ringmaster told the crowd, "Elephants, as you can see, are much bigger than pigs."

For more about punctuating direct quotations, see page 85.

Capitalize the first letter of the first word after a colon if it begins a complete sentence.

Remember that old saying: An apple a day keeps the doctor away. (But too many apples can give you indigestion!)

The rule above is actually optional. Some writers capitalize the first word after a colon if it begins a complete sentence, and some don't. However, never capitalize the first word after a colon if it does not begin a full sentence.

Remember to bring all your stuff to the picnic: bug spray, a blanket, the map, and food, food, food!

Colons

A colon looks like two periods, one on top of the other.

Use a colon to introduce a list after an independent clause (a clause that can stand alone as a sentence).

> In the animal doctor's secret trunk I found many wonderful things: three peacock feathers, a bottle of horse pills, two ostrich eggs, and the skin of a rattlesnake.
>
> We have several issues to discuss at today's student government meeting: the dress code, the soda machine, and the gum-chewing rule.

For special emphasis, you may put just one item, not a whole list, after a colon.

> After six months on the space station, the astronaut craved only one thing: a hot bath!
>
> The principal gave the students the best gift in the world: an extra day of vacation.
>
> When his invention won the company's top prize, he got the reward he was hoping for: a bigger lab.

Do not use a colon after any form of the verb *to be* ("are," "were," etc.) or words like "such as" or "consisted of."

The reasons he was expelled from school are flipping peanut butter sandwiches up to the ceiling and letting the plug out of the swimming pool.

I love all kinds of desserts, such as pecan pie, strawberry shortcake, and fruit tarts.

The contents of Tom Sawyer's pocket consisted of bits of toys, marbles, and trash.

Her happiest days were her graduation, her wedding, her daughter's birthday, and the day her dog had pups!

Use a colon to introduce a long direct quotation.

Sojourner Truth (1797–1883), a freed slave, traveled the country speaking in favor of giving women the right to vote. At a women's rights convention in Ohio in 1851, she said: "That man over there says that women need to be helped into carriages, and lifted over ditches, and to have the best places everywhere. Nobody ever helps me into carriages, or over mud-puddles, or gives me any best place! And ain't I a woman?"

If a direct quotation is very long (more than four or five lines), you should indent it and not use quotation marks. (For more about punctuating direct quotations, see *Direct Quotations* on page 85.)

Use a colon between the chapter and verse numbers when referring to the parts of the Bible.

Genesis 1:7 (This refers to the Book of Genesis, Chapter 1, Verse 7)

Luke 3:12

John 2:15

Psalms 22:3

Use a colon between the volume and page number when referring to large works (several books on one subject) or periodicals (like magazines, newsletters, and newspapers).

> *Encyclopedia Brittanica* V:325 (This means "volume 5, page 325" of the encyclopedia)

Use a colon after the greeting (salutation) to a formal or business letter.

Dear Board of Directors:	Dear Complaint Department:
Dear Sirs:	Dear Editor:
Dear Madam:	Gentlemen:
To Whom It May Concern:	My dear Senator Potter:

Use a colon after headings in a memo.

> To: Latoya
> From: José
> Date: July 19, 2001
> Subject: The Charity Walk-a-thon

Use a colon to separate the hours from the minutes when you write the time of day.

> 2:14 a.m.   7:19 p.m.

You can also use a colon to separate minutes from seconds.

> Karen finished walking around the reservoir at exactly 8:14:41 a.m., so she wins.

Use a colon to separate the parts of a ratio.

> The model of the city was built on a scale of 100:1.
> There's a 19:1 ratio of students to teachers at this school.

The Student Council passed the no-homework rule by a 3:1 vote, but the teachers said, "Forget it!"

Use a colon to separate a heading or an introductory label from the words that follow it.

HELP WANTED: Alligator Wrestler

HEADLINE: Man Falls Into Eyeglass Machine, Makes Spectacle of Himself

SIGN OVER THE PRINCIPAL'S DOOR: "Abandon Hope All Ye Who Enter Here"

CAUTION: Wet Paint (really wet!)

IMPORTANT NOTICE: School ends at 1:00 p.m. today.

Use a colon to separate the names of characters from their lines in the script of a play.

JOSEPH: Can you help me hang this picture I just painted?

HELENE: It's beautiful. What is it?

MRS. RUSSO: It looks like spaghetti and meatballs.

(There are several ways of punctuating a play script. See *Play Scripts* on page 89.)

Use a colon to separate the title from the subtitle of a book.

Monsters and Creatures: My Life as a Sixth-grade Teacher

Bad Bard Barred: Censoring Shakespeare's Plays

Commas

Commas are the most overused, underused, and abused punctuation marks in the English language. People don't put enough commas into their writing, or they put in way too many, or they put them into the wrong places. Here is how to really use commas correctly.

Put a comma between independent clauses of equal value when there are three or more, and they don't have commas in them.

> Katie bought the food, Tommy cooked the meal, and Sue washed the dishes.

Put a comma in front of a coordinating conjunction to join two independent clauses in a compound sentence.

> Independent clause, conjunction independent clause.

The words that follow the comma + conjunction could be a complete sentence by themselves.

(For definitions of *independent clause, coordinating conjunction,* and *compound sentence,* see the Glossary starting on page 92.)

> Leonard went to see a romantic film, and Harriet went to a science-fiction movie.
> Lorrie gave Al a computer for his birthday, but he really wanted a teddy bear.
> Help me clean up the kitchen before Mom gets home, or I will tell Cindy that you like John.

You don't need the comma if the clauses are very short:

> You pitch and I'll catch.
> A cow moos but a canary tweets.
> Stop it or he will throw up.

Do not put a comma between two or more verbs that have the same subject. (That's a compound predicate, also called a compound verb, not a compound sentence.)

> subject   verb   verb
> David loves computers and got a job as a computer artist.

Use a comma only if the second verb has its own subject.

> subject   verb   subject verb
> David loves computers, and he got a job as a computer artist.

Put a comma after a dependent clause that comes before an independent clause in a complex sentence. **(See pages 93 and 92 in the Glossary for definitions of** *dependent clause* **and** *complex sentence*.**)**

A dependent clause at the beginning of a sentence begins with a word like *after, although, because, if, since, when, while,* etc.

> When Misty appeared on
>   the cover of a cat
>   magazine, he got calls
>   from pet modeling
>   agencies.
> Although I spoke
>   French to my
>   stuffed monkey, he
>   still spoke English
>   back to me!

If I drop this strawberry pie on your head,
  will you be grateful or angry?
Because there were rocks in my bed, I
  didn't sleep well.

If you reverse the order of the clauses—and put the main clause first—don't put a comma after the main clause.

I didn't sleep well because
  there were rocks in my
  bed.

**Put a comma between
two adjectives**

1. when they describe the same noun, and
2. the word *and* could be put between the adjectives without changing the meaning.

the fat, feathery parrot (the fat *and* feathery parrot)
an adorable, smart kid (an adorable *and* smart kid)

Do not use a comma between two adjectives if the second adjective and the noun go together as if they were one item. Test: If you put *and* between the adjectives, it would not sound right. For example: torn wedding gown. "Torn *and* wedding gown" sounds wrong, so don't use a comma between the adjectives.

chocolate birthday cake	roasted chicken sandwich
huge Sunday dinner	battered straw hat
red brick house	baggy bell-bottom pants

**Put a comma after an adverbial
phrase at the beginning of a sentence.**

An adverbial phrase is a group of words (without a subject and a verb) that does the job of an adverb. (This phrase usually modifies a verb and answers the questions How?, Where?, or When?)

> At the top of the erupting volcano, nobody spoke. ("At the
>   top of the volcano" answers the question "Where?")
> During the horse race, he shouted himself hoarse. (When did
>   he shout? During the race.)
> With unexpected courage, she addressed the creature. (How
>   did she speak? With courage.)

You don't always have to put a comma after a beginning phrase if the phrase is very short. It's your choice.

> At dinner we ate all the desserts before the main course.
> Before sunrise the bullfrogs croak in harmony.

Do not put a comma after a beginning phrase if the word after that phrase is a verb.

> verb
> Out from under the bushes slithered the deadly snake.

> verb
> In those rusty tin cans were the treasures of the sultan.

**Use commas to set off nonrestrictive phrases and
clauses. These phrases and clauses give information but
are not really essential to the meaning of the sentence.**
(See page 94 in the Glossary for the definition of *nonrestrictive*.)

> Wah Seiu, who lives in Walla Walla, has his own Web site.

The main point of the sentence is that Wah Seiu has his own Web site. The fact that he lives in Walla Walla is not necessary to the main point, so put commas around those words.

Do not use commas to set off restrictive clauses. **(See page 94 in the Glossary for the definition of *restrictive*.)**
Think about these two sentences:

> The burglar who had stolen the queen's crown was caught.
> The burglar, who had stolen the queen's crown, climbed
>   noiselessly out of the palace window.

In the first sentence, only the burglar who had stolen the queen's crown was caught. If you left out "who had stolen the queen's crown" (the restrictive clause) you wouldn't know which burglar was caught. (There could have been more than one burglar.) "The burglar was caught" is not specific enough. So do not put commas around "who had stolen the queen's crown."

On the other hand, the meaning of the second sentence is that the burglar climbed out of the window. You could take "who had stolen the queen's crown" out and the rest of the words would still tell the reader the main point of the sentence: the thief escaped. Therefore, put commas around the words that are not essential.

Put a comma after words like *oh*, *yes*, and *no* at the beginning of a sentence.

> Oh, you were the person inside the gorilla costume.
> Yes, I will marry you, but only on a Thursday morning.
> No, and I would appreciate it if you stopped whistling.

**Put a comma after the close of any letter
(personal or business, friendly or not).**

Sincerely yours,	Love,
Yours truly,	Disgustingly yours,
Best regards,	Furiously,
Warmest wishes,	With great annoyance,

Put a comma after the greeting of a personal letter.

Dear Aunt Paula,   Dear Joan and Ed,   Hi, Max,

(Put a colon after the greeting of a business letter. See page 39.)

**Use a comma to avoid confusion
(by making the reader pause slightly).**

To Lester Shirley was a
    beautiful woman.
To Lester, Shirley was a
    beautiful woman.

Shortly after the carnival
    shut down.
Shortly after, the carnival
    shut down.

**Use a comma to separate
two of the same words
(that might cause confusion
next to each other).**

Miriam rolled on on her new roller
    skates.
Miriam rolled on, on her new
    roller skates.

Monroe strolled in in his usual casual manner.
Monroe strolled in, in his usual casual manner.
When the money ran out out ran Mango.
When the money ran out, out ran Mango.

Use a comma to separate three or more items in a series (including before the conjunction and the last item).

Pa bought potatoes, peaches, peppers, and peanuts.
She got an A+ in something: math, science, or history.
The hippo was short, chubby, and frowzy, but incredibly light
  on his feet, and when he danced the ballet, he was amazing!

You may notice that some writers don't put a comma in front of the conjunction and the last item in a series. That's OK, but the use of this comma is becoming more and more popular, and it really helps separate all the items very clearly.

Use a comma in front of a direct quotation that is not at the beginning of a sentence.

Mrs. Scotto said softly, "The math test tomorrow has a
  thousand problems on it. Class dismissed."

Use a comma at the end of the first part and in front of the second part of a direct quotation that is divided up in a sentence.

"The math test tomorrow," said Mrs. Scotto softly, "has a
  thousand problems on it. Class dismissed."

Note that the first comma comes before the first closing quotation mark and the second comma comes before the second opening quotation mark. (See *Direct Quotations* on page 85.)

Put a comma after the last word of a direct quotation

1. that is a statement, not a question or an exclamation.
2. that is not divided up.
3. that is not the last thing in the sentence.

"The math test tomorrow has a thousand problems on it,"
said Mrs. Scotto softly. "Class dismissed."

(See *Direct Quotations* on page 85).

**Put a comma before and after a nonrestrictive phrase, clause,
or word that comes between the subject and the verb.**
(See page 94 in the Glossary for the definition of *nonrestrictive*.)

This city, founded in A.D. 124, was sacked by the Visigoths.
The Latin teacher, who's been here since the day the school
opened, must be about a hundred years old.
My sisters, however, both live north of Boston.
Your name, I'm sorry to say, is too long for the telephone
book, Mrs. Van Hinkletinklepickleticklefootsietootsie.

**Use commas to set off a noun of direct address
(the person who is being directly spoken or written to).**

At the beginning of a sentence, use one comma:

Peter, don't do that disgusting thing that you always do.

In the middle of a sentence, use two commas:

Don't do that disgusting thing, Peter, that you always do.

At the end of a sentence, use one comma:

Don't do that disgusting thing that you always do, Peter.

Use commas to set off appositives.

An appositive is

1. a noun (or noun phrase)
2. that comes after another noun (or noun phrase)
3. and gives additional information about it.

An appositive can come *in the middle of a sentence:*

noun   appositive

Dr. Soghoian, the headmaster of our school, never shouts.

An appositive can come *at the end of a sentence:*

noun

One person who never shouts is Dr. Soghoian, the

appositive

headmaster of our school.

Do not use commas with a restrictive appositive. An appositive is called *restrictive* if the meaning of the sentence would be changed, incomplete, or confusing without it.

The playwright William Shakespeare wrote over thirty world-famous plays.

The words *William Shakespeare* are *restrictive* because if you left them out, the reader would not know who the playwright was, so no commas are used.

Mark Twain's book *Huckleberry Finn* is banned in some schools.

You have to include the name of the book. If you didn't, the reader wouldn't know which of Twain's books is banned. It's definitely needed (restrictive), so do not put commas around it.

Use commas to set off official titles and important positions. These titles and positions are like appositives.

> Mad Ludwig, King of Insania, lived in a fantastic castle at the peak of a slippery slope.
> One of the few women heads of state at that time was Golda Meir, Prime Minister of Israel.
> Hubert J. Figglesworth, Ambassador from Pontovia, broke his eyeglasses and couldn't read his speech.

Use commas to set off expressions or words that break the flow of thought at the beginning or in the middle of a sentence.

> Well, I didn't realize he was seven feet tall when I said I would go out on a date with him.
> Monday, after all, is the first day of the rest of your life.
> The storm started, of course, just as the picnic began.
> We had no choice, therefore, but to kick the statue.
> At that time, however, the goat still lived in the house.

Use a comma before and after words and abbreviations like *namely*, *i.e.*, and *e.g.* when they are used to introduce an example or a series of things.

Note: *i.e.* and *e.g.* are the abbreviations of Latin phrases.

> i.e. means "that is to say" (Latin: *id est*)
> e.g. means "for example" (Latin: *exempli gratia*)

They are usually used only in more formal kinds of writing, like research reports, not in everyday papers. Sometimes they are printed in italics.

After working on her invention for two years, she treated herself to a hiatus, i.e., a break.

He never forgot to bring a treat for her puppy, e.g., a bone or an old sock.

They love their new school for a lot of reasons, namely, the terrific kids, the great teachers, and the food in the lunchroom.

Use commas to separate parts of addresses and places when they are written in a sentence.

She lived at 20 Joyce Road, Peabody, Massachusetts, until she moved to 51 Grove Street, Lynn, Massachusetts.

My full address is 325 Jarvis Street, Littleville, Iowa, United States of America, North America, Western Hemisphere, Earth, Solar System of the sun Sol, plus my zip code.

Put a comma after the day of the week, after the number of the day, and after the year when the sentence continues after the year.

They were married on Sunday, June 20, 1965, while flying over the Pacific Ocean in a hot-air balloon.

> On July 4, 1776, the Declaration of Independence was adopted by the Second Continental Congress.

A date can have four parts to it:
1. the day of the week (Monday, Tuesday, etc.)
2. the month (January, February, etc.)
3. the number of the day on the calendar (1 to 31)
4. the year (44 B.C., A.D. 881, 1941, 2003, etc.)

When you write a date, you do not have to use commas if the month and the year are the only two parts you are writing.

> She was born in July 1976.

But if you are writing *three or more* parts of a date, you must put commas after the name of the day, the number of the day, and the year unless the year is the last item in the sentence. Never put a comma between the month and the number of the day.

> On Monday, July 19, 1976, she was born.
> She was born on Monday, July 19, 1976.
> She was born on a Monday in July 1976.

Use commas to set off *etc.*

Etc. is the abbreviation of the Latin phrase *et cetera* and means "and so forth." It always has a period after it.

When *etc.* comes at the end of a series, put a comma in front of it. When the sentence continues after *etc.*, put a comma both before and after it.

> The coach told me I had to show up on time, never miss a practice, get my uniform cleaned, put the equipment away, etc., or he would drop me from the team.

If *etc.* is the last word in the sentence, put a comma before it but no comma or extra period after it.

> I had to get the ball, the bat, the net, the score cards, etc.

If *etc.* is the last word in a question or in an exclamatory sentence, put a question mark or exclamation mark at the end, as usual. Don't forget the period after *etc.*

> "Do I have to feed the animals, wash the car, shovel the snow, etc.?"
>
> "Yes, feed the animals, wash the car, shovel the snow, etc.!"

Compound Words

Compound words are two or more words used together as nouns or adjectives (sometimes even as verbs). They can be written three different ways:

1. all one word (called *closed* compounds)
2. two separate words (called *open* compounds)
3. two or more words connected by a hyphen (called *hyphenated* compounds). For more about hyphens, see page 60.

Most compound words are written as one word, but you can't always be sure, and there are no rules to help you. Some words can be written more than one way. Examples: folktale, folk tale, and folk-tale. So if you're not certain if a compound word is one word, two words, or hyphenated, look the word up in a dictionary or check it on your spell check. If there's more than one way to write it, take your pick.

COMPOUND WORDS

One word	Two words	with a hyphen
basketball	air conditioner	All-American
battleship	back talk	brother-in-law
campfire	box seat	free-for-all
classroom	eye shadow	good-looking
firehouse	half brother	hard-boiled
grasshopper	lawn mower	Italian-American
horseshoe	dry cleaner	old-fashioned
washcloth	field glasses	out-of-bounds
wristwatch	blood pressure	up-to-date

Dashes

A dash is a straight horizontal line that is longer than a hyphen. Type two hyphens in a row (without touching the space bar) to make one dash. (The hyphen key is usually the third key from the right on the top row of a computer keyboard.) On some computer word processing programs you can insert a dash as a special symbol without having to type two hyphens. Check your instruction manual.

Use a dash before and after words that show a break in thought.

A writer sometimes interrupts his or her thought to give an example, a definition, or an additional fact. Sometimes the writer wants to make an unexpected comment. The sentence continues after the second dash.

> The greatest scientific developments of the twentieth century—space travel, computers, satellites—are nothing compared to the invention of disposable diapers.
> He paid a huge amount—over a million dollars—for that antique car, but I thought it was an ugly junk box!
> According to the teacher—but not any of the students—the 206-page reading assignment was easy.

Use a dash to show that a speaker has been interrupted.

> The detective announced softly, "The name of the murderer is—" But before he could finish his sentence, a shot rang out.
> When she won the lottery, she shouted, "I can't believe—" and fainted flat on the floor.

Use a dash to give extra emphasis to an appositive. (See *appositives* on page 49.)

> The little man waiting in line to buy
>   ice cream is Gustav—the Emperor
>   of Slobovia!
> She fell head over heels in love with
>   El Flippo—the world's greatest
>   trapeze artist. He swept her off her feet!

Use a dash in front of the name of the person who wrote or said something that you are quoting.

> "Do not wait for leaders; do it alone,
>   person to person."   —Mother Teresa

> "The best way to cheer yourself up is to try to cheer
>   somebody else up."   —Mark Twain

> "Men are like the stars. Some generate their own light while
>   others reflect the brilliance they receive."
>   —José Martí

(See "Hyphens and Dashes: What Are the Differences?" on page 60.)

Ellipses

An ellipsis is a series of three dots in a row. The dots are the same as periods on a keyboard. The plural of "ellipsis" is "ellipses."

Sometimes you may want to use just part of a quotation in the paper you are writing. You are allowed to cut words out of the quotation, but you must put dots in to show where the missing words used to be. Put a space before and after each dot in the ellipsis.

Use three dots to show that words have been left out at the beginning of or inside a quoted sentence.

Here is a quote from Helen Keller:

> "I have depended on books not only for pleasure and for the wisdom they bring to all who read but also for that knowledge which comes to others through their eyes and their ears."

Now here is that same sentence cut almost in half. An ellipsis takes the place of the missing words in the middle of the sentence.

> "I have depended on books . . . for that knowledge which comes to others through their eyes and their ears."

Use three dots to show where a person paused, hesitated, slowed down, or changed thoughts while speaking.

> Chook Houng was so surprised that she could hardly speak. She stammered, "I don't know what to . . . this is the greatest honor I could ever . . . I never thought I would win a . . . thanks very much," and then she sat right down.

Use a period plus an ellipsis (a total of four dots) to show that the words you left out came at the end of a quoted sentence.

Put a period right after the last word you quote with no space between the word and the period. Then add three more dots with a space before each dot.

> Lincoln said, "Four score and seven years ago our fathers brought forth upon this continent, a new nation...."

Use a period plus an ellipsis (a total of four dots) to show that a whole sentence, more than one sentence, or a whole paragraph has been left out of a quotation.

Lincoln's Gettysburg Address is 268 words long. Below is an example of how it could be cut to just 125 words using ellipses.

At Gettysburg Lincoln said:

> Four score and seven years ago, our fathers brought forth upon this continent, a new nation... dedicated to the proposition that all men are created equal. Now we are engaged in a great civil war testing whether that nation... can long endure. We are met on a great battlefield of that war. We have come to dedicate a portion of that field as a final resting place for those who here gave their lives that that nation might live.... The world... can never forget what they did here.... It is rather for us to be here dedicated to the great task remaining before us... we here highly resolve... that government of the people, by the people, for the people shall not perish from this earth.

Exclamation Points

Exclamation points are sometimes called exclamation marks.

Use an exclamation point at the end of an exclamatory sentence that is full of strong feelings (like joy, fear, anger, horror, or surprise).

She loves me! She loves me! Who *is* she?
I'm going to be a banana in a television commercial!
The dam has burst! Evacuate the city!

(See *Sentences* on page 91.)

If a direct quotation is an exclamatory sentence, the exclamation point goes inside the closing quotation mark.

She threw open the door and shrieked, "My fake diamond is
    missing!"

(See *Direct Quotations* on page 85.)

Extra: In Spanish, an exclamatory sentence is written with two exclamation points: an upside down one at the beginning and a regular one at the end.

¡Se quema mi casa! (My house is on fire!)
¡Gané la lotería! (I won the lottery!)

Put an exclamation point after a strong interjection at the beginning of a sentence.

Yikes! The pickle truck turned over in the middle of town.
Wowza! That's some gigantic pumpkin.
Yippee! We won the Purple Pines Ping-Pong Play-offs.
Iccch! That's revolting.

Hyphens

A hyphen is a short, horizontal line. (The hyphen key on a keyboard is in the top row, on the right, just to the left of the = key.)

HYPHENS AND DASHES: WHAT ARE THE DIFFERENCES?

A hyphen is half the size of a dash. (When you type, two hyphens equal one dash.)

A hyphen is used *inside a word*.

A dash is used *between words*.

Use a hyphen to connect parts of some compound nouns. (See Compound Words on page 54.)

son-in-law
self-awareness
tractor-trailer

Different writers don't always hyphenate words the same way. For instance, some authors use "vice-president" and "teen-ager," and some prefer "vice president" and "teenager." All are correct. If you're not sure if the compound word you want to use is hyphenated or not, look it up in a dictionary you trust or check it on your spell check.

Use a hyphen to connect parts of a compound adjective that comes in front of the noun it is describing.

Do not use a hyphen in a compound adjective that comes after the noun it describes.

When the compound adjective comes before the noun, use a hyphen.

adjective   noun

Please don't wear that moth-eaten sweater again.

When the compound adjective comes after the noun, do not use a hyphen.

noun   adjective

The sweater she wore to school was moth eaten.

Adjective comes before the noun (use a hyphen):

adjective   noun

Many state-of-the-art products were invented here.

Adjective comes after the noun (do not use a hyphen):

noun   adjective

All the products invented here are state of the art.

Do not use a hyphen when the first part of a compound adjective is an adverb that ends with *-ly*.

The freshly washed clothing blew
   off the line.
The newly minted dollar bills
   looked counterfeit.

Use a hyphen to form adjectives with *well* when the adjective comes in front of the noun it is describing (but never when it comes after).

He was given a well-deserved award for his bravery.
His award for bravery was certainly well deserved.

The well-bred gentleman tipped his hat to the lady.
A man who tips his hat to a lady is well bred.

A well-expressed phrase is a delight to read.
It's a delight to read a phrase that is well expressed.

His mother is a well-known rocket scientist.
His mother, the rocket scientist, is well known.

Use a hyphen with *-elect*.

Adding *-elect* to a word means that a person has been elected to an office but has not yet actually taken that office. For instance, a person is President-elect of the United States in the time between the election on the first Tuesday in November and the inauguration the following January 20th.

Mayor-elect, Governor-elect, President-elect

Put a hyphen in a compound word between a prefix and a proper noun or an adjective.

mid-July festival
non-European food
pro-Middle East peace
anti-Nazi protest
un-Shakespearean language

Use a hyphen between syllables when you have to break a word into two parts because you ran out of space at the end of a line.

The movie was stupid, but it was the most hilar-
    ious movie that I ever saw. I just couldn't stop laugh-
    ing for an hour afterward. But it was definitely stu-
    pid.

Don't divide one-syllable words at the end of a line. Don't leave just one or two letters at the end of a line or at the beginning of the next line. If you are not sure where the break between the syllables comes, look the word up in a good dictionary.

Use a hyphen to join numbers from twenty-one to ninety-nine when the numbers are written as words.

As a general rule, all numbers from one to ninety-nine should be written out as words in your written work. Numbers starting with 100 may be written as numbers.

> Jade Ping graduated from business college when she was twenty-one, and by the time she was thirty-two, she owned 104 computer repair stores.

Use a hyphen to join the parts of a fraction when it is written out as words.

> two-fifths   three-sixteenths   five-eighths

Do not use more than one hyphen to write out fractions.

> two sixty-fourths of an inch   three thirty-seconds of a mile

Use a hyphen between the parts of a compound adjective

1. that contains words and numbers that are written as numbers.
2. when the adjective comes in front of the noun it describes, not after.

The 10-mile "Fun in the Sun" race was canceled because of snow.
His 89-year-old grandmother did push-ups in the barn.

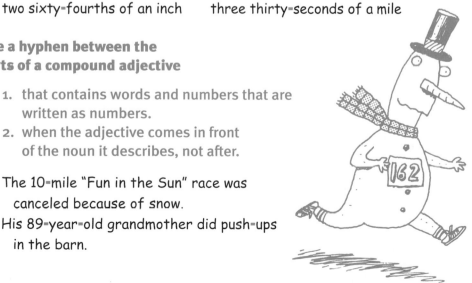

Roger Bannister was the first person to run a 4-minute mile.
An 8-foot-tall woman married a 4-foot-tall man and had
6-foot-tall children.

Use hyphens when you spell out a word for emphasis.

I want this filthy, that's f-i-l-t-h-y, room cleaned up
immediately!
When I say *no,* I mean no! N-o. No!
"You spell *hippopotamus* h-i-p-p-o-p-o-t-a-m-u-s," said the
teacher.

Use a hyphen in double last names.

Some people's last names consist of two last names connected by
a hyphen.

Ms. Youngman is married to Mr. Oldman, and their kid's last
name is Youngman-Oldman!
Wanda Wozensky-Polensky lives in Kadensky.

Use a hyphen after a prefix to avoid confusion between some words.

recreation (fun and games)
re-creation (creating something again)

recover (to get back, regain)
re-cover (to cover something again)

coop (an enclosure for birds)
co-op (a short form of the noun *cooperative*)

remark (to make a comment)
re-mark (to mark again)

Put a hyphen after some prefixes like *ex-*, *self-*, and *all-*, especially if the last letter of the prefix is the same as the first letter of the word it's connected to.

anti-inflammatory   ex-mayor

re-enact   pro-feminist

all-loving   self-supporting

If you are not sure when to use hyphens with prefixes, look the words up in a dictionary or your spell check.

Put a hyphen between places, years, times, numbers, pages, etc., that mark limits. (The hyphen is often a substitute for the word *to* between the items.)

During the 1999-2000 school year, the score of the Chelsea-Everett Thanksgiving Day football game was 27-26!

(There is a hyphen between "Chelsea" and "Everett" to show that the game was limited to those two teams.)

The Middle Ages (approximately A.D. 500-1500) were sometimes called the Dark Ages, but that's not a good name.

Read pages 122-145 for homework.

We are open Monday-Saturday, 8 a.m.-6 p.m.

Indenting

When you indent, you set the first word of a line in from the left margin.

Indent at the beginning of each new paragraph.

If you are using a word processor, indent about five spaces from the left margin by hitting the space bar a few times or by hitting the tab key once. Indent about one inch if you are writing your paper by hand.

> One of the most famous speeches ever given in the twentieth century is Dr. Martin Luther King, Jr.'s, famous "I Have a Dream" speech. He delivered it on August 28, 1963, standing in front of the Lincoln Memorial in Washington, DC, in front of hundreds of thousands of people at a civil rights rally. The speech was broadcast on television that day, and it has been replayed many times since, most notably on Martin Luther King Day every January.

Not all writers indent the first sentence of each new paragraph. Sometimes in business letters and in some books, writers skip a line between paragraphs without indenting. That's another way to show the reader where one paragraph ends and the next one begins. It's your choice, but if you do indent, be consistent. Do it throughout your paper.

Indent all lines of a long quotation.

If you are quoting more than four or five lines from a poem or from any other source, indent all the lines ten spaces from the left margin if you are typing or using a word processor. Indent all lines approximately two inches from the left margin if you are writing. Don't use quotation marks if you indent a whole quoted passage.

> Rain, rain, I hate to complain,
> But you are driving me insane;
> I thought I had made it perfectly plain,
> That I didn't want you here again;
> So please abstain, oh rainy rain,
> From raining on my windowpane;
> Thank you.

At the back of your elbow in your upper arm is a bone called "humerus" in Latin. "Humerus" sounds like "humorous," so many years ago people started calling that bone the "funny bone." If something makes you laugh, people say that it "tickles your funny bone." That is the origin of that famous idiom.

What did the invisible kid call his mom and Dad? Transparents!

Italics

Letters that slant to the right are in italics. Most word processing programs on computers allow you to type in italics when you want to.

Use italics for titles of

magazines: *The New Yorker* operas: *The Marriage of Figaro*
newspapers: *USA Today* musical shows: *Fiddler on the Roof*
books: *Freedom's Children* movies: *Jurassic Park*
plays: *Death of a Salesman* television shows: *Seinfeld*
radio programs: *All Things Considered*

You can also underline these titles instead of putting them into italics. See the section on underlining on page 80.

Use italics for stage directions in the script of a play.

JENNIFER: (*hysterically throwing her plate on the floor*) I will never eat meat again! Never! Never!

Stage directions in a script of a play can be printed in italics with or without brackets or parentheses. It depends on who is writing or typing the script. (See *Play Scripts* on page 89.)

Use italics to emphasize a word for special effect.

She asked him to marry her?
She asked *him* to marry her?
She asked him to *marry* her?
She asked him to marry *her*?

Do you see how changing the word in italics changes the feeling the writer is trying to express in each of the sentences above?

Parentheses

A parenthesis is one upright line that curves either to the right or to the left. Two of them together are a pair of parentheses.

Use a pair of parentheses to enclose any extra words that you put into the middle or at the end of a sentence of your own (not a sentence you are quoting) that add details or explanations.

These words usually interrupt the sentence and are not as important as the rest of it, but they do add extra information which may be useful or interesting.

> Each of his six brothers (whose names all begin with J) has a long, curly mustache.
> I'm going to the Student Planning Committee (which organizes bake sales and dances) to bring up my idea.
> It was the longest baseball game ever played (see the sports records on page 27), but everyone stayed until the end.
> The high school (also known as the "prep school" or "upper school") is located at 4 West 93rd Street.

Put a pair of parentheses around a whole, separate sentence that you put into a paragraph to add extra details, facts, or explanations.

Punctuate the separate sentence in parentheses just as you would any other regular sentence.

> The summer camp I go to is in Maine. It lasts from the end of June through the end of August. (It gets freezing cold at night in Maine in August!) The camp has sports, drama, arts and crafts, and swimming.

Put a pair of parentheses around numbers or letters that list items in a series.

> These are the things she did today: (1) milked the cows, (2) fed the chickens, and (3) plowed ten acres. And that was before breakfast!
> Before you can get the job, you must do the following: (a) Fill out an application form.
> (b) Pass a physical exam.
> (c) Have an interview.

Use a pair of parentheses around a question mark after a word or statement to show that you are not sure if the fact you are stating is true or 100 percent accurate.

> My great-great-grandma became mayor in 1876 (?) when she was almost ninety years old!
> She beat her opponent in the election by 2,000 (?) votes.

(See *Question Marks* on page 73.)

You can also use parentheses in the script of a play to enclose stage directions that are typed in italics. This shows the actor what he or she should do, not say.

> JENNIFER: (*hysterically throwing her plate on the floor*) I will never eat meat again! Never! Never!

Stage directions in a script can also be put into brackets or just printed in italics. It is the choice of the person writing or typing the script. (See *Play Scripts* on page 89.)

Periods

Put a period at the end of a sentence that states a fact, makes a comment, or expresses an opinion.
(See "Declarative Sentences" on page 91.)

> Tuesday is the best day because I eat lunch early.
> A guppy is a little fish, but it can have hundreds
>   of babies.

Put a period at the end of a mild command or a request.
(See "Imperative Sentences" on page 91.)

> Print your name neatly at the top.
> Please stop doing that.
> Will you pass the peas, please.

The last sentence may sound like a question, but it's really a request and should have a period after it, not a question mark.

When an order or command is strongly worded and full of emotion, put an exclamation point after it. (See *Exclamation Points* on page 59.)

> Stop doing that!   Be quiet!   Halt!

Put a period after abbreviations.

There are hundreds of abbreviations that are followed by periods. Here are a few of the most common:

> Ms. Diana, Mrs. Addelston, Dr. Sherman, Gen. (General)
>   Powell, Capt. (Captain) Lew

44 B.C. (or B.C.E.), A.D. 1099 (Note: A.D. goes in front of the year.)

4:28 p.m., 8:14 a.m. (Note: a.m. and p.m. may also be written as A.M. and P.M.)

Jan. (January), Feb. (February), Aug. (August)

Sun. (Sunday), Tues. (Tuesday), Wed. (Wednesday)

Shurtleff St. (Street), Stanwood Rd. (Road), Columbus Ave. (Avenue), Sunset Blvd. (Boulevard)

Smith & Co. (Company), the science dept. (department)

B.S. (Bachelor of Science), M.F.A. (Master of Fine Arts)

Not all abbreviations have periods. The following do not:

the official U.S. Postal Service abbreviations for the fifty states (FL, MA, CA, NY, TX, etc.)

some company names (CBS, MTV, IBM, AT&T, etc.)

some sports organizations (NFL, NBA, etc.)

some government agencies (NASA, FBI, CIA, etc.)

Some writers put periods in abbreviations where others don't. For instance, U.S.A. can also be written as USA. If you are not sure about putting periods in an abbreviation, look it up in a dictionary.

Put a period after numbers or letters in a list printed vertically (one item on top of another).

To finish the project, you'll need:
1. three rubber chickens
2. a football helmet
3. six pigs' tails

Put a period after initials in people's names.

Susan B. Anthony   Michael J. Fox   E. B. White

Question Marks

Put a question mark at the end of a direct question.

> Is your name Miss Kleinman?
> How many miles are there in a light-year?
> If you crossbreed a tiger and a lion, do you get a tion or a liger?

Note: Do not put a question mark after an indirect question. An indirect question does not repeat the exact words of the question. It is really a statement, not a question.

Indirect question (no question mark at the end):

> She asked me where the hat with the turkey feathers is.

Direct question (question mark at the end):

> Where is the hat with the turkey feathers?

Put a question mark at the end of a declarative sentence that you make into a question without changing the order of the words. This kind of question expresses the feeling "I can't believe it!"

> She kissed my little brother?
> He ate the whole super-jumbo pizza by himself?
> That weird woman with the green hair is the princess?
> You want *me* to take you to the dance?

When you are not positively sure of a fact, put a question mark inside a pair of parentheses after the fact. (See *Parentheses* on page 69.)

> Someone in his family—his great-great-grandfather (?)—was the general during the War of the Dancing Toads.

Do not use a question mark at the end of a mild imperative sentence (see *Sentences* on page 91). It may sound like a question, but it's really a request.

> Will you please help me up the stairs with this stuffed brontosaurus.

In Spanish, a question is written with two question marks: an upside-down one at the beginning and a regular one at the end.

> *¿Cómo se llama tu muñeca?* (What is your doll's name?)
> *¿Qué día es hoy?* (What day is today?)

Quotation Marks

**Put quotation marks around all
the parts of a direct quotation**

1. at the *beginning* of a sentence:

   "Your homework for tomorrow is to build a medieval castle
   out of sugar cubes," said the history teacher.

2. in the *middle* of a sentence:

   The history teacher said, "Your homework for tomorrow is to
   build a medieval castle out of sugar cubes," and the class
   cheered.

3. at the *end* of a sentence:

   The history teacher said, "Your homework for tomorrow is to
   build a medieval castle out of sugar cubes."

4. that is *split up* in a sentence:

   "Your homework for tomorrow," said the history teacher, "is
   to build a medieval castle out of sugar cubes."

(See *Direct Quotations* on page 85.)

Put quotation marks around the titles of

   songs: "My Old Kentucky Home"
   chapters in a book: "The Neighbors from Outer Space"
   episodes in a television show: "Helen's First Job"
   articles (in a newspaper, newsletter, or magazine): "Kids
   Today—Angels or Devils?"

poems: "The Road Not Taken"
speeches: "I Have a Dream"

(See *Underlines* on page 80 and *Italics* on page 68 to learn how to punctuate the names of the books, newspapers, magazines, shows, etc., that these songs, stories, chapters, and articles come from.)

**Put quotation marks around words or short phrases
that are unfamiliar, unexpected, ironic, or sarcastic.**

Because he was almost seven feet tall, they nicknamed him
   "Shorty."
Chi-Ho always called me "odious," and I thought he was being
   nice until I found out it meant "disgusting and rotten."
I got lost, came late, spilled soda on my new dress, and got
   sick from the food. It was a "great" party!

You can also put these words into italics for special effect. (See *Italics* on page 68.)

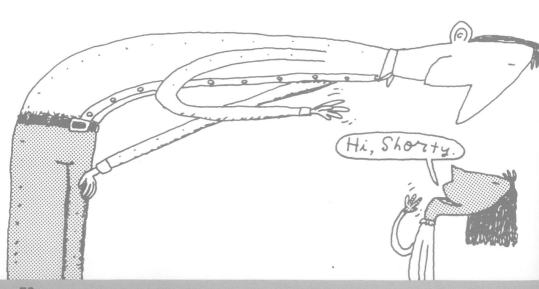

Hi, Shorty.

Semicolons

A semicolon looks like a period on top of a comma.

Use a semicolon to connect independent clauses that are not joined by a conjunction in a compound sentence.

Remember, each independent (main or principal) clause could be a sentence by itself. In a compound sentence, the independent clauses must be related in meaning.

Independent clause; independent clause.

Laurie loves to read and cook fancy dishes; Glenn writes mystery novels and works in his garden.

You can also punctuate this kind of compound sentence without a semicolon. Use a comma + conjunction instead. (See *Commas* on page 41).

Laurie loves to read and cook up fancy dishes, while Glenn writes mystery novels and works in his garden.

Put a semicolon before certain conjunctions or other connecting words and phrases that join independent clauses in a compound sentence. (Put a comma after the conjunction.)

Independent clause; **connecting word or phrase,** independent clause.

(See the Glossary starting on page 92 for the definitions of unfamiliar terms.)

Here are some of the conjunctions and other connecting words and phrases that are punctuated this way in compound sentences (semicolon before—comma after).

accordingly	furthermore	on the contrary
also	hence	on the other hand
as a result	however	otherwise
besides	in addition	that is
consequently	in fact	therefore
for example	indeed	thus
for instance	moreover	yet
for this reason	nevertheless	

Carlos was rich; however, he took the subway to work.

Mitchell loved all his birthday presents; for this reason, we won't have to return any.

Lourdes paid for the gas; therefore, she should get to drive.

Put a semicolon between series of phrases or clauses that have commas in them.

The artist got out paintbrushes, a canvas, an easel, and his palette; he set up the oranges, apples, and plums; and he painted one of his most beautiful pictures, *Happy Fruit*.

The semicolons in the sentence above separate parts of the sentence and help the reader to understand that the painter performed three different actions: he got things out, he set them up, and he painted a picture.

Anita auditioned pianists, trombone players, and flutists for her orchestra; an up-and-coming new comedian, a juggler, and a novelty dance team for her television show; and a pitcher, catcher, and outfielder for her baseball team.

Because there are so many commas in the sentence above, the semicolons are necessary to help the reader organize all the information into three separate groups of people being auditioned: (1) for the orchestra, (2) for the television show, and (3) for the team.

Slashes

A slash is an up-and-down line that slants to the right. It is sometimes called a "forward slash."

Use a slash between lines of poetry when you quote two or three lines from a poem in a regular paragraph.

Put quotation marks at the beginning and end of the quote. Put slashes between the lines of poetry. Leave a space on either side of the slash.

> In her tragic poem "Farewell, My Alien," Consuela Schlepkis wrote: "When you looked up in the sky / And I saw your extra eye / I just had to say good-bye!" Could anything be more heartbreaking than that?

Put a slash between words used in pairs.

> either/or   pass/fail   and/or   he/she

Put a slash between numbers in a fraction.

> $^1/_4 + {}^1/_4 = {}^1/_2$

Use slashes to separate parts of an Internet address.

> http://lcweb.loc.gov/exhibits/gadd/ga.html

> This is the Internet address for the Library of Congress's Web site on Abraham Lincoln's "Gettysburg Address."

Underlines

Underline the titles of

magazines: <u>National Geographic</u>
newspapers: <u>Bigelow Bugle</u>
books: <u>The Wind in the Willows</u>
plays: <u>Romeo and Juliet</u>
operas: <u>Madame Butterfly</u>
musical shows: <u>The Sound of Music</u>
movies: <u>Titanic</u>
radio programs: <u>The Story Hour</u>
television shows: <u>60 Minutes</u>

If you write on a computer with a word processing program that has italics, you can italicize the titles above instead of underlining them. It's your choice. (See *Italics* on page 68.)

Part Two

2

KINDS OF WRITING AND THE PUNCTUATION MARKS THEY USE

Bibliographies

When you do research for a paper, you can look in books, magazines, newspapers, or on the Internet. You may search for information on a CD-ROM, or you may even interview someone. At the end of your paper, you must tell where you got all your facts. A bibliography is a list of all the sources you used to write your paper. The bibliography contains important facts, such as the names of authors, the titles of books, and publishing information (where the book was published, who published it, and when).

Each item in a bibliography must be punctuated in a certain way. Here are the ways to punctuate the most common sources for a research paper.

When you list several sources in a bibliography, list them in alphabetical order by the author's last name or by the first word in the entry. Indent all lines after the first.

Note: None of the bibliographical entries given as examples below is real. They are all made up. The titles that are in italics in the entries below could also be underlined without italics.

Book:

You must always give three pieces of information about a book you used: author or authors (followed by a period), title of book (in italics or underlined, followed by a period), and publishing information (followed by a period).

Here is how to list a book written by one author.

Author's last name, Author's first name. *Title of book.* City of publication: Name of publisher, Date of publication.

Banter, Nej. *Fantastic Jewelry Designs.* New York: Silversmith Publishing, Inc., 1976.

If there are two or three authors, list the first author's last name and the name(s) of the other author(s) in regular order.

Two authors:

> Jordan, Sandra, and Mike L. Angelo. *What's Under the Paint.* Rome: Easel Books, 1929.

Three authors:

> Taraban, Samuel, Sara Gillets, and Albert Katz. *Our Wonderful Son.* Chelsea, MA: Shawmut Books, 1940.

If a book has more than three authors, write just the first author's name (last name, comma, first name) and the Latin words **et al.** (which means "and others") for the other authors. The rest of the entry is the same as for books by one, two, or three authors.

> Norfox, Harry, et al. *Punctuation Drives Me Crazy.* Chicago: Punc Publishers, 1998.

Magazine Article:

> Author's last name, Author's first name. "Title of article." *Name of magazine.* Volume number (if any). Date of publication: Page number(s).

> Sculing, Barbara. "Wacky Laws I Have Often Broken." *United States Official Law Journal.* July 22, 2000: 320–322.

Newspaper Article:

> Author's last name, Author's first name. "Title of article." *Name of newspaper.* Date of publication, Section and page number.

> Manushkin, Fran. "Great Animals of the Bible." *The Chicago Gazette.* Nov. 2, 1999, G 44.

Personal Interview:

> Last name of person interviewed, First name of person interviewed. "Personal interview." Date of interview.

> Lerangis, Peter. Personal interview. Aug. 19, 1998.

The Internet:

When you do research on the Internet, give as much information in your bibliography about your source as you can. Put angle brackets (< >) around the Internet address. (It's a good idea to print out the material you are using. It may not still be available on the Internet if you have to find it again.)

> Author's last name (if given), Author's first name (if given). "Title of article." Internet: <Internet address> Date you got the information.

> Bryant, Bonnie. "Horses With Their Saddles Off." Internet: <http://www.whinnyandneigh.com> May 21, 2000.

Computer Software (CD-ROMs, Disks, etc.)

> Author's last name (if given), Author's first name (if given). *Title of software*. Computer software. Name of publisher, Copyright date or date of publication. Type of software (CD-ROM, disk, etc.).

> Levine, Ellen. *Adventures on 101st Street*. Computer software. Koedt Edutainment, 2001. CD-ROM.

Direct Quotations

A direct quote (or quotation) repeats the *exact words* a person said or wrote.

There is a difference between direct and indirect quotations. (See *indirect quotation* in the Glossary on page 93.)

Direct (use quotation marks):

Harriet told me, "I love living in New York City."

Indirect (do not use quotation marks):

Harriet told me that she loves living in New York City.

Here are twelve good rules about punctuating direct quotations.

1. Put quotation marks around the direct quotation (the exact words that came out of a person's mouth).

Cindy said, "Take Jade to the store with you, John."
"Where's Ashley's book?" Dennis asked Lynda. "I can't find it anywhere."

2. Capitalize the first word of a direct quotation.

Jessica told Aaron, "That's a great haircut you got."

3. If the direct quotation is broken into two parts, don't capitalize the first word of the second part (unless it's a proper noun, a proper adjective, or the pronoun I).

"Shana, my dear sister," whispered Sasha, "where is my favorite blue skirt?"

4. If the direct quote is broken into two parts, put a comma at the end of the first part (before the first closing quotation mark) and another comma before the second opening quotation mark.

> "Stan, will you wear your chicken costume when you go golfing," asked Helene, "or should I put it in the laundry?"

5. Put a comma before the first quotation mark (when the sentence does not begin with the direct quotation).

> Zach shouted to Zoe from the top-floor window, "Where did you hide the dog?"

6. Put a colon after an independent clause that introduces a quote (especially if the quote is four or more lines long and is formal, such as in a research paper, official report, or business letter).

> Bonnie's announcement to the crowd was shocking: "Kurt and I are eloping tonight! Saddle the horses. Cancel the wedding. Notify the press. Stand back. Don't try to talk us out of it. Our minds are made up!"

7. If the sentence continues after the direct quote, you may end the direct quote with a question mark, an exclamation mark, or a comma, but not a period. Use a comma instead of a period. (A period can come only at the end of a sentence.)

> She asked, "Is that me?" and started to cry.

She screamed, "That isn't me!" and her face turned scarlet.

She murmured, "That's me," and quickly walked away.

8. If the direct quote comes at the end of a sentence, the final punctuation mark before the closing quotation mark may be a period, question mark, or exclamation mark, but not a comma.

He whispered, "That's my train."

He asked, "When does the train get here?"

He shouted, "I missed my train!"

9. If the direct quotation is long (with four or more sentences or many words), do not use quotation marks. Use a colon to introduce the quotation. Indent the whole quotation about ten spaces or two inches from the left. Leave two lines blank both before and after the quotation.

My favorite part of the Declaration of Independence says:

When, in the Course of human events, it becomes necessary for one people to dissolve the political bands which have connected them with another, and to assume among the powers of the earth, the separate and equal station to which the Laws of Nature and of Nature's God entitle them, a decent respect to the opinions of mankind requires that they should declare the causes which impel them to the separation.

10. When you quote what someone said or wrote, and it is more than one paragraph long, put opening quotation marks at the beginning of each paragraph. Put closing quotation marks only at the end of the whole quotation, not at the end of each paragraph.

The great Native American Chief Hiawatha spoke to the leaders of five Native American nations in the 1500s. He was trying to convince them to stop fighting among themselves and unite. He said:

"You, the people sitting in the shade of the great tree whose roots dig deeply into the earth and whose branches spread far and wide, shall be the first nation because you are fearsome and powerful.

"And you, the people who rest yourselves against the eternal, immovable stone, shall be the second nation because you always provide wise guidance.

"And you, the people who have your home at the foot of the great mountain and are shaded by its projecting rocks, shall be the third nation because you are all highly skilled in speaking."

The speech worked. The five nations formed the Iroquois Federation.

11. When you quote a conversation between two or more people, start a new paragraph every time a different person starts to speak.

"Which cat knocked over the vase of flowers," Karen asked, "Tiger or Peaches?"

Fatima answered, "I think it was Peaches."

"How can you tell?" asked Franklin.

"Because," said Fatima, "Tiger is pointing an accusing paw at Peaches. And Peaches looks guilty."

"Aaarrgh!" growled Peaches as she ran away.

12. Use single quotation marks to enclose a quote within a quote.

Loraine told me, "I heard the zookeeper say, 'The gorilla has escaped!' but I really didn't believe it until I felt this hairy hand on my shoulder."

Play Scripts

When you write a play, there are several ways to write the name of the character who is speaking, the stage directions (what the actor is supposed to do), the words the actor should say, and the way he or she should say them. You can use capital letters, lowercase letters, italics, parentheses, brackets, periods, colons, boldface, and spacing in different ways. Any way that you write out a script is fine as long as the actors can understand clearly what they are supposed to do and what they are supposed to say and not confuse the two. Here are the most common ways of writing scripts. Choose one that looks good to you, and remember to be consistent. Use the same punctuation throughout your play.

CARMEN. (*Jumping up and down.*) Hello, Mohammed.

Rozzie
[*Jumping up and down.*] Hello, Juan.

MADELINE
(*Jumping up and down*)
Hello, Malcolm.

ASHLEY:
   Jumping up and down
Hello, Raphael.

Rosa [*jumping up and down*]. Hello, Denzel.

TAMIKA [*Jumping up and down*]: Hello, Marilyn.

Sentences

There are four kinds of sentences. The chart below shows what they are called, what they do, and what punctuation mark to put at the end of each. Examples follow.

Kind of sentence	What it does	Final punctuation mark
Declarative	States a fact or makes a comment	Period
Interrogative	Asks a question	Question mark
Imperative	Gives a command or makes a request	Period (for a request or a mild order) or an exclamation mark (for a strong command)
Exclamatory	Expresses a strong emotion	Exclamation mark

Declarative:
He was born on Valentine's Day.

Interrogative:
Does his sister design unusual jewelry?

Imperative:
Pass the lizard sauce, please.
Put that tooth down this minute!

Exclamatory:
The jelly-making machine exploded!

Pass the lizard sauce, please.

I would, but I don't have any arms.

Lizard Sauce

Glossary

GLOSSARY OF GRAMMAR TERMS USED IN THIS BOOK

In order to understand how punctuation marks help make writing clearer, you have to know a little grammar. These are the meanings of the grammar terms in this book.

abbreviation: a shortened form of a word.

abstract noun: a word that names something that exists but that you can't actually see, touch, taste, hear, or smell (like freedom, justice, love, or happiness).

adjective: a word that describes or modifies a noun or pronoun and answers questions like What kind of? How many? and Which one(s)?

adverb: a word that modifies verbs, adjectives, or other adverbs and answers questions like How? When? Where? and To what extent?

adverbial phrase: a group of words without a subject and a verb that does the job of an adverb.

appositive: a noun that comes after another noun and gives additional information about it.

bibliography: a list of sources that were used by the writer of a research paper, article, or book.

clause: a group of words that contains a subject and a verb.

complex sentence: a sentence that is made up of one or more independent clauses and one or more dependent clauses.

compound adjective: an adjective made up of two or more words (joined together as one word, used as separate words, or connected by a hyphen).

compound noun: a noun made up of two or more words (joined together as one word, used as separate words, or connected by a hyphen).

compound sentence: a sentence that is made up of two or more independent clauses.

conjunction: a word that joins words, phrases, or clauses together.

contraction: a word made by putting two other words together and leaving out a letter or letters. (An apostrophe is put where the missing letters were.)

coordinating conjunctions: the linking words *but, or, yet, so, for, and,* and *nor.* (To help remember them, think of "boys fan.")

declarative sentence: a sentence that states a fact or makes a comment.

dependent clause: a clause that cannot stand alone as a sentence by itself (also called a "subordinate clause").

dialogue: a conversation between or among people.

direct quotation: the exact words a person says.

etc.: the Latin words *et cetera,* which mean "and so forth."

exclamatory sentence: a sentence that expresses a strong feeling or emotion (fear, horror, surprise, etc.).

formal: in this book, describes a serious paper (like a history research report) that is written according to strict rules of grammar, punctuation, etc.

imperative sentence: a sentence that gives a command or order, or makes a request. (The end punctuation mark is either a period or an exclamation point, depending on the intensity of the sentence.)

indent: to leave space between the left margin and the words.

independent clause: a clause that can stand alone as a sentence by itself (also known as the "main" or "principal" clause).

indirect quotation: words that express someone's thoughts, feelings, questions, or ideas but do not exactly repeat the person's own words.

informal: in this book, a paper written according to less strict rules of writing (like a fairy tale, story, play, letter, diary, etc.).

initial: the first letter of a word.

interjection: a word that expresses a strong feeling or emotion (usually followed by an exclamation mark).

interrogative sentence: a sentence that asks a question.

italics: letters that slant to the right.

main clause: a group of words with a subject and a verb that can stand alone as a sentence (also known as the "independent" or "principal" clause).

memo: a brief note to someone about a specific subject.

nonrestrictive: describes any phrase or clause that is not essential to the meaning of a sentence. (The phrase or clause could be left out and the main point of the sentence would still be clear.)

noun: a word that names a person, place, thing, or idea.

noun of direct address: the person (and sometimes the thing) being directly spoken to or written to.

phrase: a group of words that does not contain a subject or a verb.

plural: more than one.

possessive: showing ownership or a very close relationship.

prefix: a word unit, made up of a few letters attached to the front of a base word, that changes the word's meaning.

principal clause: a group of words with a subject and a verb that can stand alone as a sentence. (Also known as the "independent" or "main" clause.)

pronoun: a word like *I, me, he, its, their*, etc., that can take the place of a noun.

proper noun: a noun that names a specific person, place, or thing (and sometimes an idea).

ratio: the relation in number or degree between two similar things. Example: There is one teacher for every fifteen students in this school, so the teacher-to-student ratio is 1:15.

restrictive: a clause or phrase that is essential to the meaning of the sentence. (If this clause or phrase were left out, the main meaning of the sentence would not be clear.)

salutation: the word or phrase of greeting at the beginning of a letter, note, e-mail, or other written correspondence.

singular: only one.

subject: the word that names the person, place, or thing that the sentence is about and that tells who or what is performing the action of the verb.

subordinate clause: a clause that cannot stand alone as a sentence. (Also known as a "dependent" clause.)

syllable: a unit of a word that consists of a single uninterrupted sound.

verb: a word that shows action, doing, or being.

Index